GW00394314

Richard Thomas is a poet from Plymouth, UK with poems and haiku published/forthcoming in *Orbis, Fire, Weyfarers, Caught in the Net, The Lake, Ink, Sweat and Tears, Neon Highway, The Coffeehouse, Lunar Poetry, Reflections, Notes from the Gean, Presence, Bottle Rockets, The Screech Owl, Carousel SW, Venus in Scorpio, Wild Orphan, Futures Trading, Tribe, Tears in the Fence* and *The IMPpress,* as well as on the websites *Clinic* and *Neutral Norway,* amongst others.

Having graduated with a First Class Honours BA in English and Creative Writing from Plymouth University, Richard now studies an MA of the same title. Richard was shortlisted for the National Poetry Competition 2011 and his first full collection of poems *The Strangest Thankyou* was published by Cultured Llama in 2012.

Previously Editor of the poetry e-zine *Symmetry Pebbles,* Richard is now the Creative Writing Editor for *Tribe,* and was Managing Editor for the 2015 issue of Plymouth University's creative writing journal *INK.* Richard is a regular performer of his work, both with and without accompanying musicians, and he has performed all over the South West, but most notably at Port Eliot Festival, Barnstaple Fringe, and Apples and Snakes' 'Forked' at The B-Bar, Plymouth; he has also performed his poetry on *BBC Introducing* for Radio Devon.

Zygote Poems is a short collection of poems that traces the journey of new fatherhood with the effects of anxiety. The collection uses phonetic language to emphasise the effect anxiety can have on a person during a particularly emotional or mentally taxing period. This comes into particular effect with numbers and dates – an overwhelming feeling arises within, and the mind fogs over, coming to a climax in the poem 'Surtralleene', a poem about the drug used to medicate the ailment, written phonetically. Such purposely mis-spelled poetry doubles up to produce 'baby language', giving effect to the innocence and development of the poet's daughter, whom these poems circle around, praise and adore. The use of the asterisk, indicative of the footnote, then pulls the poems together.

Zygote Poems is as engaging as it is starkly honest, grappling in equal measure with the anxieties and charms that come with new fatherhood. Thomas' poems offer a guide through the mundane intimacy of daily routines, from dirty nappies, to tinned pineapples, to newly cut teeth, as the richness of language and wordplay veer away from easy sentimentalities to confront the very real challenges (and joys) of holding on to one's own emotional strength as they take responsibility for another.

Angela Szczepaniak
Lecturer in English and Creative
Writing, Plymouth University

for Emmeline

I would like to thank my family and friends for their support creatively and personally, my daughter Emmeline for blessing me with her presence, and Angela Szczepaniak for mentoring me through the process of this collection.

Some of these poems have previously appeared in *The Poetry Kit*'s 'Caught in the Net', *Ink, Sweat and Tears, Futures Trading, Lunar Poetry, Reflections* and *The Screech Owl*.

ZYG✳TE
POEMS

Other books by the author

The Strangest Thankyou (Cultured Llama, 2012)

ZYG✳TE
POEMS

RICHARD THOMAS

Cultured Llama Publishing

First published in 2015 by
Cultured Llama Publishing
11 London Road
Teynham, Sittingbourne
ME9 9QW
www.culturedllama.co.uk

A CIP record for this book is available from The British Library

ISBN 978-0-9932119-5-9

Printed in Great Britain by Lightning Source UK Ltd

Jacket design by Mark Holihan

Author photo by Harry Chi Li

Contents

Zygote Poem

At Twehn-tee Wonn & Twehn-tee Ate
it's poppy seed making itself at home,
and then it's apple seed fashioning
intestines – brain – lungs – heart – liver,
it's sweet pea running the* juices around,
sweet pea expanding to blueberry,
neurological surface grows,
raspberry comes, a seasoning berry,
limbs in frantic wading and waving;
and then it's all ears wide open,
the green olive makes audible the pulse,
prune or date or fig in its placement
stirs mechanisms up to whirling,
lime is the turning point of man from sea,
toes and fingers unwebbed and parted,
plum swelling to globular peach,
all systems are flowing animation,
and the emerging tools to eat and speak,
the lemon is keen to peel,
kidney, spleen and liver unravelling,
spinning then from citrus to citrus,
all legs from the navel orange,
how avocado comes and it's all top,
the budding of lashes, brows and hair,

onion hardens the skeleton,
hoarding fat for the long journey ahead,
when the sweet potato is sweetening,
movement's felt flicking the palm,
bold is the mango like a blobbed full moon,
paints skin with vermix caseosa,
as banana elongates,
gender is confirmed and fully formed,
pomegranate filled with tasting seeds,
buds realising potential,
papaya is hazy, the sleeping fruit,
it goes dozing for Forhtean hours,
the rounded whole of the grapefruit
is all ears for throbbing and voices,
the cantaloupe getting cramped now
and nipples and face to emerge,
cauliflower is a lovely flower,
it's pulling the compass from North to South,
up and down in its lettuce state,
the peepholes mounding into position,
it's rooted as a rutabaga,
working the bustle of the brain,
and development of the aubergine
fitting its armour for the outside,

acorn squash now toughening
with hiccups skipping on the pubic bone,
a cucumber's plenty enough strength
to clasp a finger or breadstick,
a pineapple is brightening the source,
ensuring touch, smell, taste and sound work,
jicama to durian fruit,
the body clock starts its occupation,
it's further skeletally solid;
a butternut squash appearing,
a more willing recipient to song,
a coconut listens close,
honeydew melon is seeping sticky,
the wisening lungs secrete surfactant,
and winter melon weirdly warmer,
the ings of suck, breath, blink and grip,
a pumpkin floats as youthful as sunshine
with all of its Innch of softest hair,
the vital life of the watermelon
puts the womb to gymnasium of limbs,
at Forh-tee the jackfruit comes ripened,
adjusted to space and climate,
squeezing muscle and tensing the bone,
making its tracks into the wild.

You Said I Can Nurture

But I'm breathless and caustic
like a seal* in a whale kitchen,
some-Tymes I struggle to swallow
and the whale does me instead,

like a seal in a whale kitchen,
I evaporate often and inhuman
and the whale does me, instead
of walking I sideways-roll,

I evaporate often and inhuman,
hardly the typical human rule
of walking, I sideways-roll,
perhaps I awkwardly hoverboard,

hardly the typical human rule
but I'm breathless and caustic,
perhaps, I awkwardly hoverboard,
some-Tymes I struggle to swallow.

Onscreen Debut

You were a memorable jellyfish
of such wholesome form,
feeling* for the exterior
of the next stage of being,
of knowing it,
having already become.

You were a seahorse for the surface,
flitting and flipping
*in captivating Clokwyze circles:
the smallest gymnast,
a shrimpy gymnast!

We'd been ever so patient
for your grace,
and we were ever so patient
to see you in techni-colour
and no longer black and white,
to see you boundlessly dimensional.

Baby, when you made
your onscreen debut,
the grass was freshly cut,
and the lambs were jumping
outside my window.

Yours Sincerely

From the thick of the fuzz came
        the thud and we knew you were
there, heart galloping like a
horse called Love's New Dream along
            the warm uterusian
steeplechase, your pulse shooting
            like a pinball, rapidly
looping your body – so small
        that your heartbeat quicker caught
            up with itself. Tiny* one,
don't be eager to overtake
        yourself, come with patience and
ease, come with calming effect
            on the world, come I know you
            will with joy, and we'll meet
 you at the other end with
        love to last Eturnitee.

Urinating Clinical

I've taken Mennee
a self-indulgent piss
in* the cubicles
of cold cubic clinics

and in the pale
of hospital lavvys,
each Wonn contrast like
it's broiled yolk on glair/

sunny duckbill on
a China plate of snow –
there is protein in
piss and there's protein in

flesh – glair's protective of
yolk and embryo,
this building's protective
of bellied babies:

I'm pissing irony,
but what's a pissing
poem to give my anyone –
if I'd spent as much

time on the real things
as I'd spent making
witticisms of my
piss, then maybe I'd

feel human – next time my
bladder twinges and
I need to go, I'll
think better of it.

She Craved Tinned Pineapple Chunks

Not only
Tesco Express,
I went everywhere,
all over
the* wet land
of Mutley Plain –
scouring,
shuffling,
peeping.
I strode
wide pavements,
I was Chief
Explorer,
I was Roald
Amundsen
of the vital
pregnant
quest.
And though
I didn't
fully
understand it,
I did it for love
and so their bellies
were full
and warm.

@ # & W×3

Would you like it in HTML?
I would like it streamlined,

            concentrated,

                       focused,

all these new things
are code enough.
Pictures, I'll have

        pictures,

               pictures

and diagrams*,
a male mind is visual after all,
or so they keep telling me.
This modern age is lofty
in trying to understand the human form
in a series of Weakly emails –
Do you want this baby in HTML

               or plain text?

          (Does the umbilical cord wrap itself
              around Times New Roman?)

In Light of Recent Mind

Tehn Fouzund meetings and
Sehvun Fouzund appointments and
all of* them at Wonnce in
                    ugly am algorithm.

I switch the light on and it's
a Snow White looking glass and
it's clear before me, it's
showing rosy details,
but in the tight throat of Nyte I'm
to feel my way to it, I'm
like a bat looking for
        its wings in deathonic Dae,

and often I'm flobbed out,
a warm glob of chewed gum to
stick to the floor, collecting
  dry clumps of coarse cat hair.

Dry clumps of coarse cat hair
stick to the floor, collecting
a warm glob of chewed gum.
Often I'm flobbed out:

wings in deathonic Dae,
like a bat, looking
to feel my way to it.
I'm in the tight throat of Nyte, I'm
showing rosy details,
it's clear before me,
a Snow White looking glass, and
I switch the light on and it's

ugly am algorithm,
all at Wonnce,
Sehvun Fouzund appointments and
Tehn Fouzund meetings.

Tu Rooms, Pt. Wonn

It was to have Tu rooms somewhere fairly central
but with a brilliance of trees and daisy caves for picnics,

for when she comes and is wanting various jams and curds
and longs to lie in the* sun blinking and pooping.

Tu rooms would have been the ideal hold until we found
     somewhere for schooling,
and we wanted a lime tree in the courtyard like a vase of
     malachite and peridot,

beneath that a permanent wise man for our own personal
     wonderings,
all of which we could see through a prism-glassed window

paned with immortality-vision and into-the-sunset future
     starlight.
For the Fyve Hundrud mark there must have been
     something surely reminiscent

of all of those things, if not exact, or a Wonn bed basement
     flat would do it,
with constant next-door scaffolding and handfuls of noisy
     neighbours –

the baby would sleep in with us and I'd put up rose-
     paisleyed bunting,
cotton-bloated elephants, Tu trunks pointing symmetrical,

and her Fthree birdy pictures so that in effect what she did
   have
was her very own room within her Mother and Father's
   room,

and that would tide us over until we found the Wonn
   proper family home.

A Closeness of Pulses

So much soup to be in Wonn fridge*
and in Wonn freezer at any Wonn time;
whenever we wanted soup we had it there
waiting in all of its worldly abundance
for our ladles and pregnant spoons,
moon-faced spoons, swollen spoons –
there were all kinds of soups
and broths and cream-ofs,
spanning every Forhf corner
of every Forhf bone and limit:

Pea Soup   Pig Soup
Charity-Goose-Dancehall Soup
Reindeer Hoof and Coriander Soup
Empty Pocket and Bus Soup
Corn and Encyclopaedia Soup
Butterbean and Clementine
Liver and Pancake
Squid and See-Saw
Milk and Marrow
Sphinx and Muffler
Goat and Glove-Box
Lighthouse   Cheese   Lion
Buffalo Broth   Crumb Soup
Cream of Candle-Curtain

Bug-hole Broth   Shoelace Soup
and Soup the Flavour of Soup Itself,
making it the most paradoxical soup,
and all of these from Zygote
to fully functioning prodigy.

I once actually made my own soup
and when I went to store it
in the Tu tier fridge I realised
that I needn't have done it –
her grandmother had us covered:
so much so that they had to start
sending it up to space to make room,
and astronauts were made redundant
and all because of soup,
and Narcissus drowned in a pool
of his own Good-Looking Soup,
and to the point that all we ever dreamt about
    was soup –
as soon as eyelids lowered
we could think of nothing but it,
Sehvun nights a Weak
our subconscious swam in soup,
a Hormonal Red Lentil and Tomato Soup,
hoping we were skirting the edge of the bowl
in the right direction and closeness of pulses.

The Shoes

Just Innchiz of blue canvas –
it makes my belly fill up
with fluff and feathers
thinking about it –

I was an easy sell
amongst the footwear,
a salesman's dream,
there was just something

about the nothingness of* them
yet the somethingness
they could achieve
with the strong leg forward,

and the glossy hearts,
candy like, glued to shoe,
in lively tones
of pink, blue and green,

and the tamest Velcro
to pull tight
around the tops
of mission-dealt bones

and silk-soft muscle and flesh,
their palm-of-the-hand
compactness –
who knew the joy of it,

the thrill of finding
the Furhst pair you'd adorn?

How Moarning Came

She bleeped and wrestled with the Nyte*,
avoiding red bulbs and gas,
I leant my lobe to the disinfected rubber,
each of her heartbeats (hers and hers)
were sent through the floor like Morse code,

as I laid like coil curled,
and my pressed cheek throbbing recipient.
Waving around catheters, the Midwife twooed,
twittered like an owl, twooed and twooed,
waving her cannula all about and twooed,

she shuffled around me and I saw her mother helpless
(but how valiant and audacious!).
It's coming now, I can see the head.
With hairs gummed to her strained brow,
glossy with the strength of a Milliunn pure,

and a heave and a breath, Sehcunds later,
Moarning made to slow-emit its light
in a Nyne Twhen-tee Fyve splayed-sun flood,
harping the room with gold string song,
and so she came, our baby, bathed softly in blood.

Exacting It

How to make a Yung man weep:

> hold you,

> > my fleshed radiator* of love,

> > so new yet

> > so familiar,

> the exact eyes

of my imagination,

> > and we sat down together

> > > for the Furhst time

> > > whilst the midwife cleaned

> your mother up,

> > and I wept

> all my best dreams

in saying your name

and feeling my finger squeezed;

the honour of putting you

in your Fuhrst garments –

to weep,

to hold you.

Delicate Muscle Maker

Delicate muscle maker,
    your cheeks flow outward,
  and the smile you bare:
    as fresh as the Furhst daisy
      to sprout from the soil for Summer.
What strength you are building*
  to settle the score,
      to separate the mixes –
    Dendranthema Grandiflorum
  from Urtica Dioica –
      it's not all flowers, this existence,

    I am Twehn-tee Fyve enough
  to inform you lovingly with that,
    but similarly I know you well enough
    to believe you'll accomplish it,
and tense each leg to the ground –
  these vines you set forward –
    to learn movement,
    to promote progress.
  Delicate muscle maker,
    the world awaits your natural advance.

Health Visitor (Shape Caller)
A Thesaurus Noun-Replacement Poem

She's a* different face every time but with
the same discourse to her tag,
she comes and goes

like a horse out of hay
and with not quite as many hooves or teeth, but
an air of worry

that she insists is minuscule,
so you begin to blow at
a normal level again,

and she brings with her profundity – Wonn
of the Furhst summits I had
with the Shape Caller was

when I wasn't properly there,
and I was informed
by outside information

of our conference –
it had been a long milk-filled Tyme-slot
and sleepwalking had become

24

an action I was taking to well –
all I can hope
is that I was suitably dressed

when I opened Home Entrance with
my sense barely open and
totally not conscious,

but capable of talking
and directing her to the mother,
may I add.

I Took Her to See Her Mother in Hospital Every Day That Weak

It was a blast of bus-stop hieroglyphs trying to read
the Tyme-table. You do the pram-shuffle, slot yourselves be-
tween old ladies who want to wake the baby up – if she's
asleep for the journey I think she prefers it, it's a
lot of patience needed otherwise, not much fun for young
blood and wonder. And I'll remember the man with the
Tu kids who gave up his seat for us with a delicate
nod because he sympathized with the whole* baby-on-the-
bus routine and was fully aware of its various
complexities and the tricks you need to learn to get
it right each Tyme – aware out of his Furhst-hand baby/bus
experience. That Weak was a gnarled bag of vibra-
tions, Daughter and I zipping buses back and forth, pockets
pressing into my thighs with the weight of day-return-
coins and I couldn't get my hands in for shreds of holey tick-

et paper. It was from outside of the Co-Op on Mut-
ley Plain, a sweep through Mannamead like a brushstroke, up
through Crownhill like a snowplough (red bus City Bus, white bus
Nicer Bus), and a swing down and around like a tetherball in-
to the pencil-shaded outer case of Derriford Hospital.

Karma

O' sun that ripens its fiery cords
beyond the cotton-thick, milk-heavy haze:
the landlord has done a family out of a home,
boo on them, those bog-horned brats,
and sun shine on, shine all over with heart*.

Aptamil

The   tub   was   almost   keg-like
and   I   guess   it's   like   flour,
the   actual   bit   of*   it;
watered   down   it's   slightly bitter
and   mostly   bottom   of   bottle,
you   get   the   technique   down,
it's   quite   egg-shaker;
in   your   Furhst   Tehn   Munths
you must have consumed as much milk
as I have consumed in my Lyfe-Tyme –
all   that   blue-plastic   scooping,
running   out   into   the   slick-chill   Nyte
at   Tu   AM   to   get   your   fix,
you   thirsty   with   those   eyelids
heavy   with   a   Milliunn   questions
and   Innewmurabul   possibilities;
Siks Munths on and I'm still picking
the powder out from beneath my fingernails,
and I know the process plenty well
to   get   my   PhD   in   it;
Will   I   teach   you   for   your   own?
Will   it   be   a   family   textbook?

Advice on Changing the Moarning Nappy

The Sehvun AM nappy is straight forward,
and I've learnt to do it as so she doesn't notice:

> •   Nyne oz of milk in her bottle
>   to wet her tongue of Moarning parchedness,
>   and whilst she's guzzling it down,
>   it's a quick un-pop of the sleepsuit,
>   a quick un-click of the baby grow,
>   a rip of the velcro,
>   feet up together in a bunch,
>   and swipe it from underneath
>   like a magician swiping the tablecloth
>   from beneath the candlelight caviar,
>   and she's none the wiser,
>   still glugging down the micro-milk,
>   and there you've got a good* heavy nappy
>   with not a bit of hassle at all.

Now, the Ate AM nappy,
that's a completely different thing:
at that point the bowels are really underway,
and there's the whirling porridge
of Wonn Ow-er previous,
and there's last Nyte's spinach-based dinner –
for the iron (she needs the iron) –
and the bowels are really moving,
and with a slight struggle
there's shit everywhere –
and the search for the ever-absent nappy-sack.

Milk Tooth

New* sounds
have erupted
from the well of her mouth,
a clink when she drinks from a glass,
a cluck.

This tooth,
for shearing and gnawing, and tusks,
though she uses it more
for chewing rice
and spoons.

Furhst Burhfdae Sohnnit

Nothing about you is Mehtrik, you are
pure, unaccustomed, whole and gentle in
your touch on your Calunderr, just as the
wind scurrying around you like awe-
gobbed mice, attending to your Duzun, is
gentle, and you are Twehllv finely read in
bold italics popping up from your sweet-
leaf Calunderr, defying Mehtrik or
systematic convention – all of the
pamphlets your mother and I read could not
define you – there's no Cloking motion, more
the tender* rabbit, tender swan, tender
dolphin swimmingly read – and you take the
Yeer as you should: under your belt it goes.

A City Road Late at Nyte

The road of amber is quiet
in the yellow light of a cleaving autumn,
and then the brain goes rattling down
in the back of a Colgate lorry,

with fluoride threatening to burst the walls
of the holding compartment – it bulges –
and for toothpaste to stream like silly string
with plenty of foghorns going off

(the wonky tooth is feeling the fur
of Furh-tean Ow-ers un-brushed),
and then the brain comes back
in the boot of a long long limo,

quite decadent and pounding,
with everything at its nerve endings
(the stretched limo is not actually there
but definitely definitely spotted),

and the red car which is a VW Polo,
compact and economically moving,
goes sprung like a blood cell
through its Wonn committed artery

as it sails on down the road,
and the heart which is bulbil-esque
begins to blossom from the blood* cell
in a whole whorl of flurry,

and the flurry is to get home to its love
(to be wrapped warm in its making,
and the new tiny heart of its creation
is the very song to come home to).

MDEC

Earls Colne, Rushden, Hillyhead, Amesbury,
I have yet to visit these places – how
so unsatisfying they'd be to me

in comparison to the floating sea
of the height of our co-existence* – how
Earls Colne, Rushden, Hillyhead, Amesbury

must be nothing to your fingers spread free,
your gentle footing that plods the cot – how
so unsatisfying they'd be to me,

and Chewton Magna, Polyphant, Sudbury –
nothing to your fair architecture – how
Earls Colne, Rushden, Hillyhead, Amesbury

have their magpies perched, pressed up to see
your head nuzzled into my bowed neck – how
so unsatisfying they'd be to me,

those places incomparable, drab, twee,
I have been to not one of them, but how
Earls Colne, Rushden, Hillyhead, Amesbury –
so unsatisfying they'd be to me.

What Made a Meal was Love

In the* corner shop I worked the list:
eggs, cream, pudding, pepper, and
tentatively so, it's such
accurate selection
which would bode that night's
meal reward –
and the post-
dinner
bath.

Tu Rooms, Pt. Tu

It must have Tu rooms and a view overlooking
the swish of the emerald salt, or looking into

a rhododendron maze - a kaleidoscope of sugar
cats – rainbow hands – bubble-specked honey blossom –

a chrysalis coated in perfect photographs
of tortoise smiles – it must be rent-free, modest

but grandly spacious with a cactus garden on the
terracotta roof, and a swimming pool out the

back filled with stars or diamonds (negotiable),
I'm ready to sign, show me the dots, or Wonn

bedroom will do to tide us over until I'm
fully qualified in my poesy and earning a steady

coin-flow, I can DIY the living room* into
Tu rooms and she'll still have her own room,

and I'll put up a string of bright hearts and Fthree
birdy pictures to tweet her into her naps, and

it'll be a home away from her usual home
        for the weekends.

As Boxes

I've got a   box
and it's the clinicalist   white
and the widest white container,
and in it there's a   gnome

    stiff with pottered   pose
    and veins of*   clay,
    with bad back as he's knelt up
    to his bed,   afraid

    of all other   boxes
    adjoined to this primary box,
    because each box is   vacant
    like a snail-less   shell-swirl

and it's too much to move   freely
from Wonn box to   another,
not tripping over tiny   jukeboxes
or purple-dotted   bowls

    or little laundry   clusters,
    so he avoids all other   boxes
    adjoined to this primary   box,
    in a botched   attempt

of avoiding spikes in the   gut
and Cowntlehss twangs in the heart,
a Clok Cownting Twehn-tee   Forh
on the roof of a sharp-dry   mouth.

37

Finance

Running drip-dry
and stone-dry of luck:

ear-creeping claw-clunk
of the cash machine:

crushing cold-flop
on the old ears:

buggered beep-beep
of the balance* burnt out:

dry squeak of
all Barclays' safes
everywhere:

clobbing clump-shut:

Student Finance England
giving no shits:

barely bed and beans:

but it's always having the Soreen,
the mature cheddar,

the tangerine segments
precisely chunked

like tri-angled suns
that makes all of it,

each stomach-wringing night,
worth it,

and watching you

trying to spoon-feed yourself
and getting it almost in.

Zygote Poems Make a Public Appearance

When I did it
 and read the poems –
        made my bare bones public –
 put my very nature
            on its cuff,
        my eyelids gathered lochs
from the meibomian glands'
        palpebral lachrymation –

            the handclap was entirely*
            canyon-worthy –
                    though triumph was fleeting,
                    thinking
            the Unee-directional spirit
            of the microphone
                would gauze a void,

        for I returned from that moment
                and got a drink
        like a midwife
            after a long Moarning
                and I didn't really
                        want a drink,
                    and I rolled a thin cigarette
            like a tightly fastened cannula
        when I gave up smoking
                Yeers ago,

                and I saw the sun
make its pink ascent
                        like an elevating embryo,
                when I could have done
            with sleep,
              and I kept grasping
          for something,
                  and Zygote Poems
      wasn't Zygote Poems
          without the Wonn true tender Zygote
    there to hear the poems.

COFFEE /ˈkɒfi/ noun

I write all my poems in coffee
    shops lately because in coffee
    shops there are people and in coffee
    there will always be a high demand,

there will always be people pouring
    in from the weepy English Spring
    for fresh cups of Multihpul variants
    of grounded*, pressed, hot coffee.
    As long as this holds up, coffee

shops will always be mandatory because
    that is generally the best place to
    get a cup of whichever pot of coffee
    you like – when I write poetry, coffee

is a most useful tool for its caffeine,
    for its soothing quality on the
    Myalgic Encephalomyelitistic
    throat and it's pulling of crowds and
    clattering conversation to hide the

fact that it is not just the coffee
    that I came for, but to get away from
    the shrill silence of being solitary
    and dud in daydreams.

Surtralleene

It'z Surtralleene,
oar behtur* stil,
Surtralleene Hydroeclawryde:

Fyve Oh,
Wonn Oh Oh,
Wonn Fyve Oh em jee,

caw &
cote-ing,
Sowdeeum Starrchh Gliycoleight,

Poleesawbeight
Ey-tee,
mihlk pelitts apeare-ring candee,

wreckamendid
doece, increesd
doece, n-greyvd 'A':

'A' = attum,
attum = mattur,
mattur = thuh knewcleeus

of Magnihffacent
Brayne-Bawl Nurvv Sentur,
dul ling the xsploeszon inn miy hedd,

it'z kar-ming ehfehckt,
it'z *fank gohd faw thatt,*
whott thuh doktur oardured:

moaturvaeshon,
gloe of fayce,
sew Twehn-tee-ouf Sehnchuree,

it'z juhst thuh ryte,
it'z juhst thuh ryte,
it'z juhst thuh ryte tihpul.

A Diet Coke Goes a Long Way
In the spirit of Frank O'Hara's sweetly candid poem

I am at odds as to why I should be here alone atop the
    grassy knoll,
sat like a real bum, real beard to match, here amongst the
    tulips and the squiggly shih tzus
that run wild like mice about my new boots, and I'm
    having a Diet Coke with myself.
I'm a cold and remote Numburh divided Wonn Hundrud
    + Fithty ways, I feel – midst growth and passing –
and I know bygones should be bygones, as the useless
    saying goes on,
and boy, does it go on and on, I am sure I have better things
    to listen to and I know a Fue good songs.
I heard the saying on the radio when I was a kid, and an
    older kid said it at a Sea Scout camp in* the Lake District –
I was really no good at the activities that weekend,
    particularly the water sports,
but at the time I considered him saying this made him the
    great Boddhidharma and looked to him for knots and
    got on with it.
But what I'm saying is, aren't my hands purposed to be
    warm when they've been for the best part lined family
    mittens? –

I just feel like the white sky that curls the sea mist to the
    South of me is telling me otherwise.
I'm a sole ranger now, it's no wonder that I listen to
    Morrissey and The Smiths daily,

and that I connect with 'Suedehead' and 'How Soon is Now?' and I did the whole quiff thing,
and I have chased up Nico and it's just not the same and I always return to 'Hatful of Hollow',
and I see now how the grass tips tickle the cruel lashing of the February wind,
and the biting air eats the drowning sea and the fishermen are on the end of the crayfish's line,
because I have that distance, that new and sardonic telescope of eyeing things better balanced,
where love and life and death and love are slightly understood, and a lot more than they used to be.
I'm here amongst the tulips and the squiggly shih tzus, having a Diet Coke with myself,
alone atop the grassy knoll, and I have a biscuit in my pocket, I was purely peckish and thought it could kill time
as I wait for visitation to turn its beautiful Ow-er into view –
she's almost walking by herself now, her shoes are tiny, and I love her, I love her, I love her –
I wait for her, so the Fthree of us: father, daughter and grandfather, can take a stroll

along the winding wave-withered front which was recently bombed by The Great Storm of Tu Fouzund & Forhtean,
but has dried up nicely in good clean paving and things still remain for us, a sweet Saturhdae.

These Things I'll Teach You

To hold on firmly to the reins of love;
to see your silvery picture on the bathroom
    wall and nod in mutual understanding;
to tamper with the rubric but know it first
    to get best success;
to split and rip any secret and turn it inside
    out;
to make all secrets segmented satsumas;
to expose the true juices of your existence
    and be unafraid;
to share each joy like a ripened fruit;
to dig the wild vaults of everything beyond
    its primary level of conception;
to get to the concrete core of all of your pursuits;
to eat well, sleep well and enjoy the insane
    multitudes and dreams of nature;
to question the owl's short beak and categorically
    hear its call;
to see every point of the Multee-angled corner
    of Tyme as opportunity;
to renovate the space of your discovery;
to renovate your renovation of the space of your discovery;
to keep renovating;
to drive, whether it's a vehicle or not;
to complacently rest as passenger when needed;
to turn love into energy;
to turn energy into love;
to turn love and energy into world leisure bliss*;

to turn the sun and moon upon themselves,
    to make them question their rivalry or see
    themselves as a team, an invincible black
    and bright force together at last;
to pull close and encompass everything that
    is vital;
to see each of every Wonn of your blessings on
    a Daelee basis;
to cherish the great atlas of ever-changing
    composition, depth and register;
to hold your fort down at any given moment
    and come through like a champion;
to favour whichever cartoon character you
    please whether it's Tom or Jerry or your
    own creation;
to leave Keats as Keats and Shelley as Shelley,
    each a separate entity of heart-ploding song;
to not worry if Donnie Darko is a myth Furhst
    Tyme around;
to dismiss each of those last things because it
    really doesn't matter;
to actually just be your own –
that's it,
                    that's it.

The seal feeling tiny
in the diagrams
of the fridge
of nyte:

radiator building
a whole heart
of good, new,
tender,
blood
co-existence:

the room of balance
entirely
grounded behtur
in bliss.

Cultured Llama Publishing
Poems | Stories | Curious Things

Cultured Llama was born in a converted stable. This creature of humble birth drank greedily from the creative source of the poets, writers, artists and musicians that visited, and soon the llama fulfilled the destiny of its given name.

Cultured Llama is a publishing house, a multi-arts events promoter and a fundraiser for charity. It aspires to quality from the first creative thought through to the finished product.

www.culturedllama.co.uk

Also published by Cultured Llama

Poetry

strange fruits by Maria C. McCarthy
Paperback; 72pp; 203×127mm; 978-0-9568921-0-2; July 2011

A Radiance by Bethany W. Pope
Paperback; 70pp; 203×127mm; 978-0-9568921-3-3; June 2012

The Strangest Thankyou by Richard Thomas
Paperback; 98pp; 203×127mm; 978-0-9568921-5-7; October 2012

Unauthorised Person by Philip Kane
Paperback; 74pp; 203×127mm; 978-0-9568921-4-0; November 2012

The Night My Sister Went to Hollywood by Hilda Sheehan
Paperback; 82pp; 203×127mm; 978-0-9568921-8-8; March 2013

Notes from a Bright Field by Rose Cook
Paperback; 104pp; 203×127mm; 978-0-9568921-9-5; July 2013

Sounds of the Real World by Gordon Meade
Paperback; 104pp; 203×127mm; 978-0-9926485-0-3; August 2013

Digging Up Paradise: Potatoes, People and Poetry in the Garden of England by Sarah Salway
Paperback; 160pp; 203×203mm; 978-0-9926485-6-5; June 2014

The Fire in Me Now by Michael Curtis
Paperback; 98pp; 203×127mm; 978-0-9926485-4-1; September 2014

Short of Breath by Vivien Jones
Paperback; 102pp; 203×127mm; 978-0-9926485-5-8; November 2014

Cold Light of Morning by Julian Colton
Paperback; 90pp; 203×127mm; 978-0-9926485-7-2; March 2015

Automatic Writing by John Brewster
Paperback; 92pp; 203×127mm; 978-0-9926485-9-9; July 2015

The Lost of Syros by Emma Timpany
Paperback; 128pp; 203×127mm; 978-0-9932119-2-8; July 2015

Short stories

Canterbury Tales on a Cockcrow Morning by Maggie Harris
Paperback; 136pp; 203×127mm; 978-0-9568921-6-4; September 2012

As Long as it Takes by Maria C. McCarthy
Paperback; 166pp; 203×127mm; 978-0-9926485-1-0; February 2014

In Margate by Lunchtime by Maggie Harris
Paperback; 204pp; 203×127mm; 978-0-9926485-3-4; March 2015

Anthologies: poetry and short stories

Unexplored Territory edited by Maria C. McCarthy
Paperback; 112pp; 203×127mm; 978-0-9568921-7-1; November 2012

Non-fiction

Digging Up Paradise: Potatoes, People and Poetry in the Garden of England by Sarah Salway
Paperback; 160pp; 203×203mm; 978-0-9926485-6-5; June 2014

Punk Rock People Management: A No-Nonsense Guide to Hiring, Inspiring and Firing Staff by Peter Cook
Paperback; 38pp; 229×152mm; 978-0-9932119-0-4; March 2015

Do it Yourself: A History of Music in Medway by Stephen H. Morris
Paperback; 400pp; 229×152mm; 978-0-9926485-2-7; April 2015

The Music of Business: Business Excellence Fused with Music by Peter Cook
Paperback; 266pp; 210×148mm; 978-0-9932119-1-1; April 2015

Ingram Content Group UK Ltd.
Milton Keynes UK
UKHW041821180623
423620UK00002B/6

9 780993 211959